HILLARY AND TENZING CLIMB EVEREST

Bob Davidson

Dillon Press
New York

First American publication 1993 by Dillon Press,
Macmillan Publishing Company,
866 Third Avenue, New York, NY 10022

Macmillan Publishing Company is part of the
Maxwell Communication Group of Companies.

First published in Great Britain by Zoë Books Limited

A ZOË BOOK

Devised and produced by
Zoë Books Limited
15 Worthy Lane
Winchester
Hampshire SO23 7AB
England

Printed in Italy
Design: Jan Sterling, Sterling Associates
Picture research: Faith Perkins
Illustrations and maps: Gecko Limited
Production: Grahame Griffiths

10 9 8 7 6 5 4 3 2 1

Library of Congress Cataloging-in-Publication Data

Davidson, Bob.
  Hillary and Tenzing climb Everest / Bob Davidson.
    p. cm — (Great 20th century expeditions)
  Includes bibliographical references (p.) and index.
  ISBN 0-87518-534-7
  Summary: Describes Edmund Hillary's and Norgay
    Tenzing's successful climb to the top of Everest,
    and the many unsuccessful attempts prior to
    that.
    1. Mountaineering — Everest, Mount (China
  and Nepal) — History — Juvenile literature.
  2. Hillary, Edmund, Sir — Juvenile literature. 3.
  Mountaineers — Great Britain — Biography —
  Juvenile literature. 4. Tenzing, Norgay, 1914- —
  Juvenile literature. 5. Mountaineers — Nepal —
  Biography — Juvenile literature. I. Title. II. Series.
  GV199.44.92-40275 E85D39 1993
  796.5'22'095496 — dc20

Photographic acknowledgments

The publishers wish to acknowledge, with thanks,
the following photographic sources:

The Alpine Club Library: 5b; Chris Bonington: 10,
21, 24, 29b; Dave Clarke: 19b; John Cleare
Mountain Camera: 4, 5t, 8 (John English), 12, 13,
14, 20t, 27t, 28, 29t; The Royal Geographical
Society: title, 7t, 7b, (David Constantine), 9t (Capt,
J. B. Noel), 9b 11t (Frank Smythe), 11b (M. S.
Smythe), 15t,15b, 17t, 17b, 19t, 22, 23t (A Gregory),
23b, 25t; Doug Scott 25b, 26, 27b,

Cover photographs courtesy of Chris Bonington and
The Royal Geographical Society (Alfred Gregory)

The publishers have made every effort to trace the
copyright holders, but if they have inadvertently
overlooked any, they will be pleased to make the
neccessary arrangements at the first opportunity.

Contents

Climbing high

At around 11:30 A.M. on May 29, 1953, two men became the first to reach the highest point in the world — the top of Mount Everest, in Nepal. The two climbers were Edmund Hillary and Norgay Tenzing. They had set out with their team nearly two months earlier. For the final stage of the climb they were on their own. They had been climbing since 6:30 A.M., from their lonely camp 27,900 feet (8,500 meters) above sea level. When the tired men saw they had made it to the top, they shook hands then thumped each other on the back in delight. **Mountaineers** had been trying to climb this mountain for 33 years and now Hillary and Tenzing had done it.

"Because it is there"

People who climb high mountains often risk their lives to get to the top.

Mountaineers can fall or be blown off the mountainside. Falls of rock and snow, called **avalanches**, can crush and bury them. Yet every year thousands of people go climbing in the mountains. They enjoy the mountains for many different reasons — the views, the sense of freedom, the excitement. Many people will say they want to get to the top of a mountain simply "because it is there."

Mountaineering

It is always extremely cold at the tops of high mountains. The temperatures are often so low that the climbers' fingers, toes, and ears can freeze. This causes an injury called **frostbite**, and many mountaineers have lost toes as a result of it. Most climbers wear special clothes to protect themselves from frostbite. They

▼ Mountaineering only began as a sport in 1786, with the climbing of Mount Blanc ("white mountain").

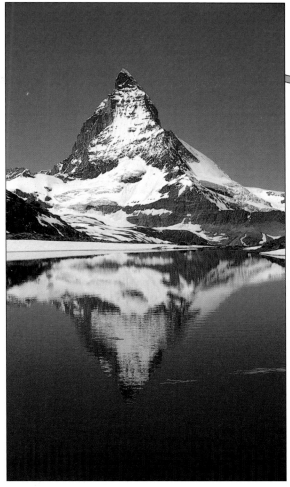

▲ The first successful ascent of the Matterhorn, in the Alps, took place in 1865.

also use equipment such as **ice axes** and **crampons** (spikes strapped to their boots) to help them to grip in icy conditions. Most mountaineers climb in teams and are often roped together to prevent falls.

When people climb in high mountains, they may have difficulty breathing. At very high levels, or **altitudes**, the air contains less **oxygen**, which people need to breathe properly. Without it, they can quickly become sick. Usually this can be prevented by climbing slowly, and gradually getting used to different conditions. This is called being **acclimatized**.

The beginnings of the sport

In 1786 a Frenchman named Michel Paccard, from Chamonix climbed Mount Blanc, at 15,771 feet (4,807 meters), the highest mountain in the Alps. Paccard's achievement created a great deal of interest in climbing mountains. Other people began to compete to be the first to climb a particular **peak**.

By the end of the 19th century mountaineers had climbed all the peaks in the Alps. They began to travel to other parts of the world to find high mountains that had not been climbed before. Mountains in Africa, the Andes (in South America), and the Rockies (in North America) were climbed for the first time. Mountaineers now thought that they had enough skill and knowledge to try to climb some of the highest mountains in the world. Some of the highest peaks are in Nepal, which has part of the Himalayan **range** of mountains.

▼ Lucy Walker (in the back row) was an early mountain climber.

The Himalayas

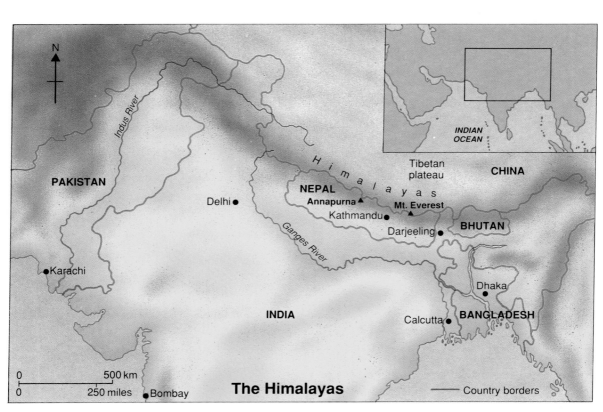

The Himalayas

0 500 km
0 250 miles

—— Country borders

The groups of mountains that lie between India and China are called the Himalayas. The word Himalaya comes from an ancient Indian language and means "snow home." The Himalayan chain of mountains is about 1,550 miles (2,500 kilometers) long and 200 miles (320 kilometers) wide. Nearly all these mountaintops, or peaks, are covered in snow all year round. Many of the peaks are steep and have jagged edges.

The high valleys in the mountains often contain ice that slowly slips downward before it reaches warmer temperatures and starts to melt. This very slow-moving ice is called a **glacier**.

The northern side of the Himalayas receives little rain and is cold. Much of this land is desert. Most of the rain in the area falls on the southern side of the mountains, and in the summer the **monsoon** brings weeks of wet weather. The southern side of the mountains is also warmer. On the lower slopes the flowers, bushes, and trees grow very quickly. Some of this land is used for farming or for growing trees.

Very few animals live in the high mountains because it is so cold and there is little to eat. Snow leopards, brown bears, and Tibetan yaks are some of the few animals that can survive in the

▲ Mount Everest is named after this British surveyor, Sir George Everest (1790-1866).

mountains. Some insects and spiders can live as high as 20,000 feet (6,100 meters).

Nepal

The country of Nepal lies to the northeast of India. Nepal's capital, Kathmandu, is in the center of the country in one of the few **fertile** areas of land. Most of Nepal is covered by the high mountains of the Himalayas. The people there live in villages scattered along the river valleys.

The highest mountain in the world, Mount Everest, is in eastern Nepal, bordering Nepal and Tibet.

Mount Everest

Mount Everest is 29,028 feet (8,848 meters) high and is surrounded by other very high mountains, with glaciers in the valleys between. The people who live near the mountain have a different name for it.

They call the mountain Chomolungma, a word used by the Tibetan people that means "Goddess Mother of the World."

The twenty-year wait

In the 1890s mountaineers turned their attention toward Mount Everest. No mountaineer had been able to get within 60 miles (100 kilometers) of the mountain to explore the area or to figure out how the mountain might be climbed. Everest could only be approached from the north, through Tibet, or from the south, through Nepal. Tibet and Nepal refused to allow any foreigners to travel through their lands, although many requests were made to the rulers of these countries. Finally, in December 1920, Tibet granted permission for one exploration in the Everest region.

▼ An aerial view showing part of the Himalayas

The north side of Everest

In 1921 a British team, including George Mallory, set out on a fact-finding expedition to Mount Everest. Since so little was known about the mountain, the aim of this first trip was to find out as much as possible about conditions in the area. This type of expedition is called a **reconnaissance**.

The team came together in Darjeeling, in India, in May 1921. The distance from Darjeeling to Everest, in a straight line, is about 100 miles (160 kilometers). However the team traveled on foot, and to avoid climbing over many mountains, they could not travel in a straight line! The route they chose meant that they would have to walk 300 miles (480 kilometers) just to reach Everest.

Walking to Everest

For several weeks they walked through rain forest, climbed river valleys, crossed mountain passes, and walked across a desert. The expedition had the help of local people to carry most of the supplies and equipment. Some of these porters were Sherpa people. The Sherpa people come from northeast Nepal and are used to mountain conditions. On June 19 they arrived in the village of Tingri, where they made their base for exploring the northwest side of Everest.

The reconnaissance

The great Rongbuk Glacier drops away northwest of Everest. George Mallory and the climbing team explored the glacier. They thought that a route to the summit might be possible from the North **Col**, but they could not reach the col from the glacier because the climb was too steep. In the end they decided that they could not approach the summit from the northwest.

The team moved their camp to the Kharta Valley. From there they explored the northeast side of Everest. In spite of bad weather, they climbed higher than

▼ Everest, seen from the Rongbuk Glacier

▲ The 1922 expedition team having breakfast

they had on the northwest side, but now they were all affected by mountain or **altitude sickness**. They climbed over the Lhakpa La Pass onto the East Rongbuk Glacier, and up to the North Col. It looked possible to reach the summit by climbing the Northeast Ridge from the North Col. However, the winds were strong, and they were all exhausted. They returned to **base camp** and the expedition ended. The team returned to England.

Climbing Everest

Immediately plans were started for the next expedition. It was to be a serious attempt to reach the summit of Mount Everest. The support team was increased, and this time there would be five climbers, including George Mallory.

On May 1, 1922, base camp was set up at the foot of the Rongbuk Glacier. The plan was to reach the North Col from the glacier, then to attempt the summit. By May 17 the team had reached the North Col, setting up three camps on the way, and set up Camp 4 at 23,000 feet (7,000 meters).

The oxygen, which the team planned to use from then on, had not arrived, and the weather was getting worse. Bravely, they decided to go on without the oxygen. The next day they reached 26,700 feet

(8,100 meters), but the wind and the cold forced them back to camp. They tried twice more, reaching 27,300 feet (8,320 meters), which was a record. Their last attempt ended in disaster when seven Sherpas were killed in an avalanche.

Disaster for Mallory and Irvine

In 1924 a third expedition made another attempt to reach the summit. The mountaineers had increased their knowledge and experience, but they, too, met appalling weather conditions. They were beaten back when they were only 1,000 feet (300 meters) from the top. The second attempt ended in tragedy when George Mallory and Andrew Irvine died high on the Northeast Ridge. Again an expedition returned home without reaching the summit.

▼ George Mallory and Major E. F. Norton in 1922, climbing on the Northeast Ridge

Expeditions in the 1930s

▲ The north face of Mount Everest. The Northeast Ridge is to the left of the summit.

Tibet remained closed to travelers between 1924 and 1932. Then another expedition was planned for 1933. Since the earlier expeditions, the design of tents, boots, and clothes had improved, so the 1933 team was better equipped than any other expedition. The leader of the expedition was Hugh Ruttledge. The number of climbers was increased to 14, and they were sure that this time they would reach the summit of Mount Everest.

The expedition followed the same route as the 1922 and 1924 teams, but they traveled earlier in the year. They reached the top of the East Rongbuk Glacier by early May. For the next three weeks, however, they struggled against **blizzards**, hurricanes, and snowfalls. Tired and exhausted, two climbers, Wyn Harris and Laurence Wager, reached 28,100 feet (8,600 meters) on May 30. The climb from this point to the summit was too hard for them. There were very steep slopes and

▲ A camp above the North Col, in 1933

they could not be sure that the surface of the snow would support them. If the surface of the snow was unstable, then their lives would be in danger. Yet again the team had to turn back, less than 1,000 feet (300 meters) from the summit.

Shipton's attempts

In 1935 a smaller British team, led by Eric Shipton, approached Mount Everest. The aim of this team was to find out whether the mountain could be climbed during the rainy, or monsoon, period of the year. Earlier expeditions had all failed because of the bad weather in the period that led up to the monsoon. Would the weather be better after the monsoon had started? Would the snow be more stable?

Shipton's team spent some weeks climbing around the north side of the mountain. They decided that an attempt on the summit during the monsoons would be too dangerous. The risk of

avalanches was higher, because the warmer weather in June and July was melting the ice and snow.

Although this expedition did not attempt Mount Everest, the members did climb 26 other peaks. It took them two months to do this. They also had another look at a possible route up Everest by the West Ridge, but they could not see a way up its lower slopes.

A full expedition in May 1936 tried the route from the North Col to the summit. They failed to make any progress above the North Col because of very bad weather, and they, too, returned home unsuccessful.

▼ Eric Shipton on the 1933 expedition

Everest from the south

There were no expeditions in the Everest area during World War II, from 1939 to 1945. In the late 1940s the religious leader of Tibet, the Dalai Lama, would not allow foreigners into the country. After China invaded Tibet in 1950, it seemed unlikely that anyone would be able to approach Everest from the north for some time.

Expeditions in 1949-1950

In 1949, however, a small British expedition was allowed to travel through Nepal, and in 1950 a French climbing team was allowed to travel through western Nepal. The French climbers made the first ascent of Annapurna, which is 26,545 feet (8,091 meters) high. Later in 1950 a team of Americans was allowed to approach the south side of Everest.

▼ The impressive summit of Annapurna

They made their way up the Khumbu Glacier to the foot of the **icefall**. The American expedition did not find out any more about the possibility of reaching the summit of Everest from the south. They did, however, succeed in getting permission to cross Nepal. This was an important step in gaining access to Mount Everest again.

The 1951 reconnaissance

In June 1951 a team of eight climbers received permission to approach the south side of Everest. This team included Eric Shipton and a New Zealander, Edmund Hillary.

The team members wanted to find out whether they could climb the icefall into the Western **Cwm**. If they could, they would then try to reach the eastern end of the cwm. From there, they would be able to see whether there was a route up the South Col and along the Southeast Ridge to Everest's summit.

The expedition traveled to Everest in September 1951. They did manage to climb, or scale, the icefall, but they were unable to go any further. The glacier in the Western Cwm was split by very large cracks, or **crevasses**, and the team could not cross them. Instead they climbed the slopes on the western side of the Khumbu Glacier, and looked up the Western Cwm above the icefall. From there, they saw that it would be possible to reach the bottom of the slopes below the South Col.

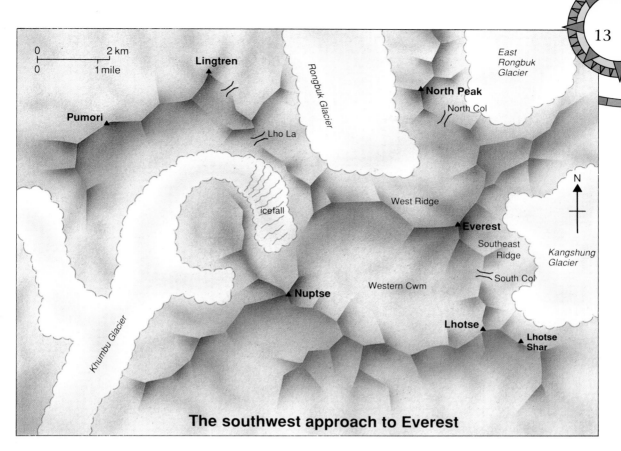

The southwest approach to Everest

When the expedition returned to England, they were sure that the icefall could be climbed and that there was a route through the Western Cwm. They were still unsure as to whether there was a route to the summit by the South Col and Southeast Ridge.

1952 — the Swiss take up the challenge

In May 1952 a Swiss climbing team took the route over the icefall and along the Western Cwm to the foot of the Geneva Spur. They climbed to the South Col and, in spite of bad weather, they climbed the Southeast Ridge to within 800 feet (240 meters) of the summit. Driven back by bad weather and lack of supplies, they had to return.

▶ A climber at the foot of the icefall

Planning the 1953 expedition

▲ The summit of Everest is to the left of the South Col, which is in the center of the skyline.

All the British expeditions to Everest were organized by a group of people who were based in London. The Everest group, or committee, was made up of members of the Alpine Club and the Royal Geographic Society. They raised the money for the expeditions from wealthy people or businesses that were interested in helping a British team to be first to the top of Everest. The *Times* newspaper was among the expedition's supporters, and the Duke of Edinburgh agreed to be the patron of the expedition.

Hunt's plan of attack

In September 1952 the Everest Committee chose Colonel John Hunt to lead the 1953 expedition. John Hunt was 42 years old, and a British soldier. He had a great deal of experience climbing in snow and icy conditions in the Himalayas. It was Hunt's job to prepare a plan, or strategy, for the 1953 expedition. It was very important to have the right plan, because the success or failure of the attempt depended on it. If the plan did not work, then not only would the team fail to reach the summit of Everest but their lives would be in danger.

Hunt felt sure that the route the Swiss team had taken in 1952 was the right one. He also knew that the key to success lay in having climbers who were properly acclimatized. They also had to have enough supplies and these had to be as far up the mountain as possible. He aimed to be at the South Col before the monsoons arrived in June. The good weather before

▲ The members of the 1953 expedition team

the monsoons usually lasted for about two weeks from the end of May to the middle of June, and in that time Hunt hoped to attempt the summit from the South Col.

This was Hunt's plan — now he had to find the climbers!

Choosing the team

Hunt needed climbers who had experience climbing in the Alps, or better still, in the Himalayas. They had to be used to the icy conditions that they would meet on Everest. They had to be very strong and fit. In addition, they had to be climbers who would make a good team and would work well together. Above all, they had to be determined to get to the top!

Hunt chose seven climbers from Britain and two from New Zealand. The British climbers were Charles Evans, Tom Bourdillon, Alfred Gregory, Charles Wylie, Michael Westmacott, George Band, and Wilfred Noyce. Edmund Hillary and

George Lowe came from New Zealand. To complete the team, Hunt selected three other climbers. Michael Ward would be the team doctor. A scientist, Griffith Pugh, would study the effects of altitude on the human body. Tom Stobart would take a film of the expedition. The money raised from showing the film would help to pay for the expedition.

A team of Sherpas would also be used to provide support for the climbers at high altitude. Hunt knew the man he wanted to lead the Sherpas. He was an expert mountaineer named Norgay Tenzing.

▼ Edmund Hillary learned his mountaineering skills climbing in New Zealand.

Choosing the equipment

Hunt was determined that the expedition would not fail because of poor equipment. He chose the best that he could find. Everything had to be light and had to work even in strong winds and the bitter cold of the mountains.

Hunt's team tested many of the latest designs in clothes, tents, boots, and

▼ The oxygen equipment was very important because it helped the climbers to reach high altitudes without becoming ill. The expedition took three different types of oxygen sets with them. The open-circuit and closed-circuit sets were for use when climbing. The third set, a sleeping set, was for use at night to help the climbers breathe properly while sleeping. The open-circuit set is shown here.

mask

cylinders

valve

sleeping bags. They decided to live on army food, which was carefully planned to give soldiers strength and keep them alive! To cook they would use 22 paraffin stoves and six gas stoves.

Mountaineering equipment

Thousands of feet of the best climbing rope, as well as ice hammers and axes, **pitons** and **snap links**, were obtained. The team needed ladders to help them cross any crevasses. One ladder was rope, and the other was made of metal and could be carried in sections. They also borrowed a mortar gun from the British army. They could fire the gun to clear any loose snow that might be ahead of them. In this way they hoped to be safe from sudden avalanches.

The oxygen equipment was most important. It had to be light and needed to last a long time. Again the climbers took the best equipment they could find.

Keeping in touch

The team took eight walkie-talkie handsets with them, so that they could talk to one another on the mountain. These sets operated up to two miles (three kilometers) apart. They also took a short-wave radio, so that they could receive weather forecasts from a radio station in India. The All-India Radio agreed to send them special weather information, which would be very important for day-to-day planning on the mountain.

▲ John Hunt testing the portable radio

Final preparations

Some of the equipment, such as the oxygen, was tested during the winter of 1952 in North Wales and in the Alps. Before leaving for India, Hunt visited Buckingham Palace and met the Duke of Edinburgh, the patron of the expedition. The duke wished the team well. On February 12, 1953, with all its equipment, the team sailed for Bombay in India.

▼ The supplies required for the Everest expedition just fit into a small field!

The 1953 expedition

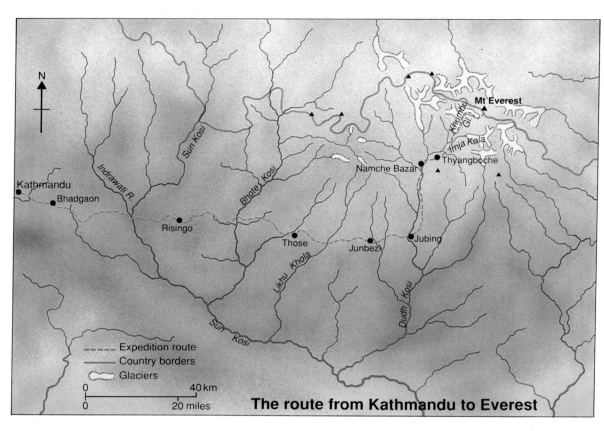

The route from Kathmandu to Everest

The expedition traveled across India from Bombay to Kathmandu in Nepal. In Kathmandu the climbers hired 350 porters to carry their equipment into the mountains. It was here that Norgay Tenzing also joined the expedition. The team left Kathmandu in early March, heading for Mount Everest.

To Thyangboche

In good spring weather the climbers walked eastward. They climbed hills and walked through woods and valleys. Sometimes they crossed foaming rivers. The countryside of Nepal is beautiful, but the walkers were thinking ahead. They knew that snow, ice, and bitter winds were waiting for them in the high mountains. On the journey they began to acclimatize to the height. They also practiced wearing oxygen masks for a few hours each day.

After seventeen days of walking the team reached the **monastery** at Thyangboche. It is more than 12,000 feet (3,660 meters) above sea level and is thought to be the highest monastery in the world. The monastery is near the Imja Kola River, which is one of the main rivers flowing south from the mountains near Everest.

▲ Members of the 1953 expedition team set up camp below the monastery at Thyangboche.

In training

Thyangboche was the team's base for three weeks of training. They needed to acclimatize properly before they began to climb Everest. So they climbed a number of mountains, up to heights of 19,000 feet (5,800 meters). They also practiced climbing together as a team and climbing with their oxygen.

The Khumbu Glacier

On April 8 the first team of four climbers left Thyangboche. This advance party followed the Imja Kola River for about 4 miles (6.5 kilometers), then they turned north. They were now in the bleak valley of the Lobujya Khola River, which flows from the Khumbu Glacier.

Their progress was slow, because new snow had fallen before they reached the glacier. They had to climb through a jumble of boulders, called **glacial moraine**, and they walked through a "forest" of tall ice spikes, or **seracs**. It took them four days to reach the foot of the icefall, at 18,000 feet (5,500 meters). There they set up camp. Several days later the rest of the expedition joined the advance party.

▼ The Khumbu Glacier

The icefall

▲ A breathtaking view of the icefall

The icefall at the head of the Khumbu Glacier is like a giant, frozen waterfall. The icefall drops steeply for about 2,000 feet (600 meters) from the end of the Western Cwm to the glacier below. There are crevasses in the ice, which change shape as the ice drops slowly. Huge icicles hang down dangerously and enormous seracs jut out from the icefall. These seracs often topple over and crash down the icefall.

Climbing the ice

Hunt could not plan a route up the slope, because the shape of the icefall changes so often. Hillary led a party up the slope and decided that the easiest and safest route lay up the middle of the icefall. There the climbers would be out of the path of avalanches that might fall from either side.

The team made slow progress up the icefall. They had to use their axes to chip out handholds and steps, and sometimes they had to cut a staircase in the ice. This would be used by those who were following with all the supplies. The team also had to build bridges across some of the wider crevasses. They used some of the sections of their metal ladder for the bridges.

After three days they reached the halfway point up the icefall and made camp on a ledge of ice. When they moved

▼ The route of the expedition through the Western Cwm and up to the summit

▲ Mountaineers in the Western Cwm heading toward the foot of the west face of Lhotse

on, there were snowfalls, which slowed them even more. It took them another seven days to reach the top of the icefall. There the team set up Camp 3, at 20,200 feet (6,160 meters).

The Western Cwm

The Western Cwm is a wild and eerie place. It is about two miles (three kilometers) long and up to one mile (1.6 kilometers) wide. It drops toward the icefall and is surrounded on three sides by mountains — Everest, Lhotse, and Nuptse. Nothing grows in the cwm, because it is so high and snow falls regularly. The cwm is split by crevasses and is bombarded by avalanches from the mountains above.

The head of the cwm

The way into the cwm from Camp 3 was split by wide crevasses. Once again the team had to use ladders to cross them. When they were in the cwm, they made good progress, leaving marker flags to show the route they had taken, in case there were heavy snowfalls. On May 1 they set up Camp 4 at 21,200 feet (6,460 meters), and two days later they reached the west face of Lhotse, where they set up Camp 5.

Camp 4 was to be the base camp for the final climb to the top of Everest. All the supplies for the next three weeks were brought up to Camp 4 by the Sherpas. They carried 45 loads, each weighing about 40 pounds (18 kilograms) over the icefall and along the cwm.

Lhotse face

The team chose a route up the west face of Lhotse to reach the South Col, and it took ten days to make this ascent. Snowfalls and high winds held the team back. They pitched two camps, 6 and 7, on ledges on the sides of the mountain, to provide support for the climbers. By May 21 they had reached the South Col and set up Camp 8.

The final ascent

Hunt planned that two teams would make separate attempts to reach the summit of Everest from the South Col. The first team was to climb to the South Summit, which was 300 feet (100 meters) below the real summit. The last stage was hidden from the South Col by the South Summit, so no one knew what the last climb would be like. If the first team reached the South Summit and was able to go on, the climbers would try to reach the top. If the team failed, the others would make the second attempt. In all, the summit of Everest is 3,000 feet (1,000 meters) above the South Col.

The climbers in the first team were Tom Bourdillon and Charles Evans. In the second team, the climbers were Edmund Hillary and Norgay Tenzing.

The first attempt

On May 26 Bourdillon and Evans left the South Col. They were followed by Hunt and Da Namgyal, a sherpa, who carried a tent, food, and fuel up the Southeast Ridge. At 27,350 feet (8,340 meters), Hunt and Da Namgyal became exhausted and returned to the South Col.

Bourdillon and Evans reached the top of the South Summit, in spite of some difficulties with snowfalls. From there they could see the final ridge, and they decided that it could be climbed. They were now at 28,700 feet (8,750 meters) — higher than anyone had climbed before.

▼ Bourdillon and Evans after their climb

▲ Hillary and Tenzing climbing up toward the Southeast Ridge from Camp 8.

However, they had neither strength nor oxygen to carry on to the top, so they returned to Camp 8. They did leave two bottles of oxygen behind, to help the following team.

The second attempt

The wind was so strong the next day, May 27, that no attempt could be made. On May 28 Hillary and Tenzing, with Lowe, Gregory, and Sherpa Ang Nima, climbed the Southeast Ridge. They collected the equipment that Hunt and Da Namgyal had left and climbed slowly to 27,900 feet (8,500 meters). Then Lowe, Gregory, and Ang Nima returned to the South Col.

Hillary and Tenzing cleared snow from the rocks and set up Camp 9. They boiled snow to make hot drinks, and as the sun set, they ate sardines, biscuits, canned apricots, dates, jam, and honey. The

apricots had to be thawed out, as they had frozen solid in the can. The two climbers then settled to sleep in the highest camp in the world.

At 4:00 A.M. they rose to discover that Hillary's boots had also frozen solid. The boots had to be thawed out over the stove, along with breakfast! By 6:30 A.M. the climbers were ready to set out. Carrying 30 pounds (14 kilograms) of oxygen equipment, they headed for the South Summit. Using their ice axes to cut steps, they reached the South Summit by 9:00 A.M. The weather was good and they had plenty of oxygen left. It was time to try to reach the summit of Everest.

▼ The summit ridge from the South Summit

The "roof of the world"

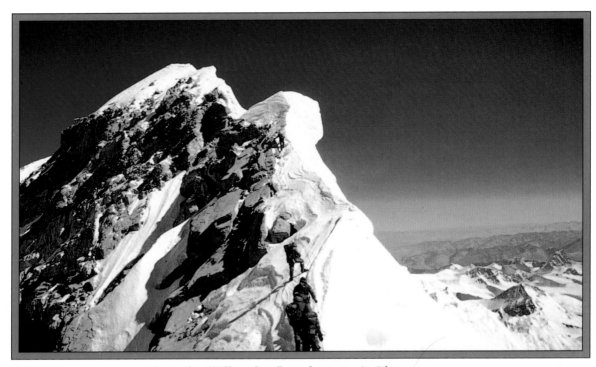

▲ Mountaineers approaching the "Hillary Step" on the summit ridge

Hillary and Tenzing climbed for about an hour beyond the South Summit. Then they came to what looked like a sheer cliff face. The cliff was about 40 feet (12 meters) high, and the rock was smooth. They did not think that they could climb up the cliff, but neither could they go around it. After some minutes of staring closely at the cliff, Hillary saw a small crack running up the side of the cliff face. He wedged himself into the crack and began to kick steps in the ice at the side of the cliff with his crampons. Slowly and painfully Hillary levered himself up to the top of the cliff. Tenzing followed him a few minutes later. This cliff is now known as the Hillary **Step**.

At the top!

Hillary and Tenzing continued along the ridge, cutting steps with their ice axes on the narrow strip of snow. The ridge seemed neverending. After two hours they were still cutting steps, and they were both tiring. After every hump in the ridge there was another, still higher. Suddenly Hillary noticed that the next hump was lower than the one he was on. They were at the top!

On the summit of Everest

Hillary said that his first feelings were of relief — no more climbing! He looked at Tenzing and knew that underneath his helmet, goggles, and oxygen mask,

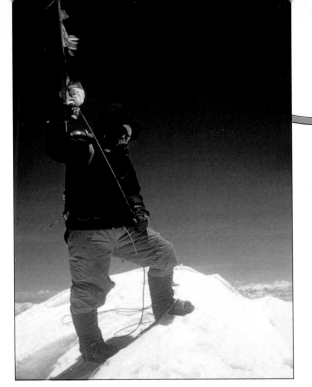

▲ Norgay Tenzing on the summit

Tenzing was grinning! The two shook
hands and thumped each other on the
back with delight. They switched off their
oxygen, took photographs, and enjoyed
the wonderful view. Tenzing made a hole
in the snow. As a Buddhist he marked the
moment by burying some small items of
food in the snow. Hillary put a small cross,
or crucifix, which had been given to him
by Hunt, into the hole.

They had reached the top at 11:30 A.M.,
and after fifteen minutes they started back
down the mountain. They picked up the
oxygen that was left by Bourdillon and
Evans, and reached Camp 9 by
midafternoon. There they melted snow
and made a sugary lemon drink — by now
they felt weak and exhausted. They
moved on down toward the South Col,
cutting steps as they went. At last, excited
but weary, they reached Camp 8 — by this
time they were almost too tired to speak.

The following day the expedition
began to leave the mountaintops.
By June 2 all the climbers were back at
base camp. From there, they returned to
Kathmandu and then to London, where
they were given a heroes' welcome in
early July. The news of the expedition's
success reached London on June 2, 1953
— the day of the coronation of Queen
Elizabeth II.

▼ A view from the highest point on earth

Later expeditions

▲ The view from the summit toward the South Summit, with Lhotse on the left

Everest has been climbed many times since the 1953 expedition. New routes to the top have been tried, often successfully. However, many climbers have died in the last 40 years while trying to reach the summit.

Breaking records

The first successful climb from the North Col was made by a Chinese team in 1960. There were 214 mountaineers involved in this expedition.

Then in 1963 an American team climbed to the summit for the first time from the West Ridge. They came down the mountain by the South Col route, which meant that they were the first team to cross, or **traverse**, Everest. Another American, Dick Bass, reached the top of Everest at the age of 55 years. He was the oldest climber to have scaled the mountain. Bass was also the first mountaineer to have climbed the highest peaks of every continent in the world.

had been tried five times before, but without success. None of the attempts had been able to cross a large band of rock, which stretches across the southwest face of Everest. Bonington planned to cross the Rock Band and at its narrowest point and to make sure that his team had enough support on the mountain.

One of Bonington's team, Nick Estcourt, finally found a way through the Rock Band. It took a great deal of courage and determination to do this. Five climbers reached the top of Everest in that expedition. Sadly, one of the climbers, Mick Burke, was trapped in a blizzard on the top and died on the descent.

▼ A camp on the southwest face in 1975

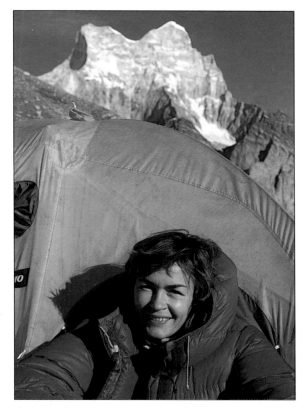

▲ Wanda Rutkiewicz

In May 1975 Junko Tabei from Japan became the first woman to climb Everest. The first European woman to climb Everest was Wanda Rutkiewicz, a Polish mountaineer. Rutkiewicz was also part of an all-women's expedition in 1985 that successfully ascended Nanga Parbat. Nanga Parbat is a mountain in the northeast of Pakistan and is 26,600 feet (8,125 meters) high.

The southwest face of Everest

In 1975 the British climber Chris Bonington led a team of climbers up Everest from the Western Cwm. This climb

North face solo

In 1980 an Austrian climber, Reinhold Messner, climbed the north face of Everest alone! He approached the summit from the East Rongbuk Glacier, then climbed to the North Col and reached the summit by crossing the north face of the mountain. Messner said that the last few feet of the climb were "agony; I have never in my life been so tired as on the summit of Mount Everest that day." Messner had to crawl these last few feet on his hands and knees.

▼ Reinhold Messner

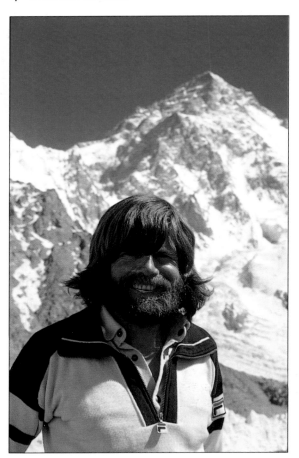

Reinhold Messner was also one of the first climbers to reach the top of Everest without using oxygen. In 1986 he became the first person to have climbed all 14 peaks in the world that are more than 26,250 feet (8,000 meters) high.

Lhotse

In 1956 a Swiss climbing team was the first to climb Everest after Hillary and Tenzing. The team went on to make the first ascent of Lhotse from the north.

Several attempts were made to climb this mountain from the south in the 1970s and 1980s, but all of them failed. Even Reinhold Messner twice failed to climb Lhotse. He called the south face of the mountain "a climb for the twenty-first century." In 1990 a young climber from Slovenia, Tomo Česen, attempted the south face of Lhotse.

Česen spent a long time preparing for his attempt. He read about other climbs on Lhotse, and he studied the south face from the mountains nearby. Finally Česen decided that he would climb alone, since he thought that it would be quicker and easier to do it that way. He also knew that to climb in daylight would be dangerous, because the sun melted the ice and caused rockfalls. So Česen climbed alone and mostly at night. After three days on the mountain he reached the top in wind and snow. He had climbed one of the most difficult peaks in the world, and he had done it alone. His success was one of the

▲ The towering south face of Lhotse

◄ Tomo Česen

greatest achievements in the history of mountaineering.

The future of mountaineering

The skill of mountaineers continues to improve. The bravery and the successes of climbers such as Mallory, Shipton, Tenzing, and Hillary have inspired many mountaineers, such as Messner and Česen. Climbers will attempt, and achieve, what was thought to be impossible. Perhaps there is now no such thing as "an impossible climb."

Glossary

acclimatize:	to become used to new conditions
altitude:	height, usually above sea level
altitude sickness:	an illness caused by the lack of oxygen in the air at high altitudes. It can be avoided by acclimatization and by drinking plenty of liquids.
avalanche:	sudden movement of large amounts of snow, ice, and stones down a mountain
base camp:	the main camp for an expedition. Food and equipment are stored here for use later on in the expedition.
blizzard:	a storm of wind and snow
col:	a dip in a mountain chain
crampon:	a metal frame with spikes, fitting the sole of the boot, for use on hard snow or ice
crevasse:	a crack in a glacier, often very deep
cwm:	an enclosed valley on the side of a hill
fertile:	describes rich soil where seeds and plants can grow well
frostbite:	permanent damage to skin caused by low or freezing temperatures
glacial moraine:	a collection of rocks, stones, and soil that is carried by a glacier for some distance and then left at the edges of it
glacier:	a "river" of ice, often several miles long, moving very slowly down a mountain
ice ax:	an ax used by mountain climbers to cut steps in ice
icefall:	a steep fall in a glacier, where many cracks and ice pinnacles develop
monastery:	a place where monks live together
monsoon:	a strong wind from the Indian Ocean that brings very heavy rain to parts of Southeast Asia at certain times of the year
mountaineer:	a person who climbs mountains as a sport

oxygen:	a gas that humans and animals need to breathe in order to stay alive
peak:	the top of a pointed mountain
piton:	a metal peg hammered into a crack in a rock to support a rope
range:	a group or row of, for example, mountains
reconnaissance:	the first trip or survey to gather information about an area
serac:	a pinnacle or tower of ice, which is often unsafe
snap link:	a metal clip used to secure a rope safely
step:	a short, steep part of a mountain
traverse:	to move horizontally or diagonally across a mountain slope. It can also mean the ascent and descent of a mountain by different routes.

Further Reading

Allen, Linda B. *High Mountain Challenge: A Guide for Young Mountaineers*. Boston: AMC Books, 1989.

Bender, Lionel. *Mountain*. New York: Franklin Watts, 1989.

Bonington, Chris. *Mountaineer: 30 Years of Climbing on the World's Great Peaks*. San Francisco: Sierra Books, 1990.

Messner, Reinhold. *Across Tibet to Mount Everest*. Seattle: Mountaineers, 1989

Reynolds, Jan. *Himalaya Vanishing Cultures*. San Diego: Harcourt, Brace, Jovanovich, 1991.

Sandak, Cass R. *Remote Places*. New York: Franklin Watts, 1987.

Index